Under Covers

Alejandra Ochoa

BookLeaf Publishing

India | USA | UK

Presentation by *BookLeaf Publishing*

Web: www.bookleafpub.com

E-mail: info@bookleafpub.com

ISBN: 9789357215145

First edition 2023

To those that believed I could.

Thank you.

ACKNOWLEDGEMENT

Thanks to those of you who have been, are, and will continue to be a part of me. There were not plenty of people who thought I could, and for the longest time, I believed them. Now as you read this small collection, I hope you know I could have never made it this far without you.

Special thanks to Mr. Daniel Herrera, no one has been such a keen witness and supporter of my growth as a writer as you. Though you were never my teacher, you met me as I was beginning my journey in writing and pushed me to pursue it. Thank you for being my friend and mentor throughout all of these years.

Practice Run

It's unfair… to find a hidden jewel.
To patiently shape and polish it,
and then be made for a fool.

Sucks to have an eye for potential.
To build one up,
then be deemed nonessential.

It's lonely... to care as would her mother.
To hold their hand as they learn to walk,
then have them run to another.

It's scary... To think that is all I can be.
A wrong turn in the right direction.
A pitstop without a fee.

It hurts... to have such good taste in men.
To love with all my heart,
but only be in chapters they need to mend.

Wake-up call

I heard its constant chime,
but I let it ring every time.

Anew

I really wish it would rain
I wish to dance in a storm
I wish to smile as it pours
I wish to soak in its showers and cry as it washes
my troubles away

I wish to hear thunder roar
I wish to feel the beat of its drums
I wish to remember what it is to live
I wish to laugh as I remind The gods that I do
not fear them

I wish to see lightning
I wish to be filled with energy
I wish for a burst of light in the darkened sky
I wish to stare upon the heavens as if my eyes
could start a fire

I wish to feel the wind
I wish to sway with the rustling leaves
I wish to be pushed by its invisible forces
I wish to breathe in the cold air and be filled
with warmth

Reborn

4

Old becomes new
as new becomes old
and the presence of time becomes unknown
as the land on which I stand disappears from
under my feet
and the world goes blank
no longer a part of me

Awakened

There came an age
When I reached a stage
where I had to turn the page
and everything I knew turned to dust
love and trust
was replaced by temptation and lust
where need
became greed
and children smoked weed
oh the look in a child's eyes
when the ones he loved shed their disguise
and everything he believed in turned out a lie
where monsters in closets no longer hide
but instead, walk among us in the outside
and without a thought
tore apart
our once innocent hearts

Intoxicated

You,
you're like poison.
Not an addiction,
or a medicine.
You're not a homemade remedy my Nana would
give me.

You're a poison.
You flow through my veins, ever so gracefully,
you settle in,
and make yourself at home.
Slowly, you penetrate deeper into me.

I mean, who would've thought -- right?
You were so sweet when you first graced my
lips,
warm, as you traveled down my throat,
kind, as you filled my eyes with darkness
rendering me blind

Blind to your toxic ways.
Blind to the decaying soul within.
Blinded by your bright colors and sweet aroma,
I let you tear down my walls,
not realizing you were burying me under them.

Personalized Engravings

Marks on your skin that retell the pains of the
past,
marks that though healed house fears
marks that bring you to tears,
marks that forbid you from seeing clear

Scars hold sorrows for tomorrow to bear
and people ask, but it hurts to share
but how could anyone compare
how do you make them understand that they had
to be there?

They had to watch the joy drain from your eyes
they had to be witness to all the lies
they had to stare as you fell and scraped your
knee on a carpet that felt soft beneath your feet

they say those marks make you unique
but how can they say that when the scars aren't
theirs to keep?
how can you make them see that though the
knife is small the cuts were deep?

Tattooed on my skin are stories whose ink has
found its way into my heart and into my dreams,

they keep me up as they play around in my head
and I lay there sinking into my bed
the thought of tomorrow now something I dread

Having been left there for dead
still unable to remember
unable to comprehend
exactly when my body turned to parchment
and how he came to hold the pen

Rose-tinted Nightmares

It was when the bines of your arms released me
from their twine that I realized they were the
glue that held me together.

It was when the puzzle piece of your lips no
longer fit with mine.

It was when you took the sun from my eyes and
filled them with rain clouds that watered the red
petechia blossoms that freckled the rounded hills
of my cheeks

It was when you slowly pulled away the heavy
blanket of your love exposing the green and
purple hues that painted my skin.

It was when you turned your back on us
no, it was when you turned your back on me that
I realized just how broken I was

Unconditioned

Slowly,
The walls I let crumble before you
Began to reassemble

And now
every time you push me farther
I let you

I let you push
And shove
And cower

I let you toy
And be coy
And pretend it gives you power

I let you run
And hide
And be sour

I let you hurt me
and overlook me
And take it by the hour

I let you remember

And be tender
And return to the love that for you I render

I let you learn
And be stern
And know that I will not surrender

Midnight Glow

The moon does not compare itself to the sun.
For the sun may rise with the land bringing
energy and vibrancy
It may shine upon the earth with intensity
Flushing the world with light
It may create warmth
and it may create life
But the moon
The moon will rise with the tide
Bringing peace and tranquility
The moon will part a sea of shadows with the
softest glimmer of hope
The moon will smile at you in the lone of the
night
And allow you to bask in its humble glory
The moon will not force its light upon you but
instead, the moon
The moon will embrace you with its gentle glow
when you have wrapped yourself in darkness

Frostbitten Roses

I fell for a vision of tomorrow
I let my heart flutter
Let my eyes gaze upon your light
And paved a path to a nonexistent future where
your soul intertwines with mine.

I set myself afire
Planted seeds of hope unaware of the seasons
Blossoms sprung open releasing their sweet
aroma into the winter air
And I fell into the warmth of your colors

I nurtured my dreams
But neglected my reasoning
I poured my love freely
and you rewarded me with a garden in the snow

But its roots soon became cold
Its petals froze
and stems dwindled
You were not ready

My clock was too fast
my ambition too wild
Flowers should come with spring

I loved you far too soon

But had I known how it would end
How it would tear me down
And push me off my cloud
I would still fall in hope
that just maybe....you'd catch me

Second Choice

15

In your sugarcoated words, I heard a ring of
truth.
Your intentions good and rooted in youth.
Your honeysuckled lips pressed to mine,
I allowed myself to forget it is she on your mind.
From your heart spills love-filled prose
but am I truly your last rose?
If she were to call your name,
would your choice remain the same?
Were I to prick my finger upon its thorn
alone would I be left to mourn?
I cannot fall again for you
for that means you I once outgrew
And though I've wallowed away in fear,
I find it helps to have you near.
In your hands, I place my trust,
any doubt now turned to dust.
So continue on the path you lead,
and I will give you all the love you need.

Discarded

And I fell,
like a petal off a wilted flower
Picked from the lavish gardens of your heart
I could no longer bask in the warmth of your
love

Meticulously Paired

You are the sun
to my moon
chaotic and bright
never letting anyone near
for fear they'll burn in your truth
and disappear

you are the earth
to my sky
keeping me grounded
as I teach you to fly
you quiver and shake
as my storms keep you awake

you are the ocean to my shore
you push and pull
in fear of your waves
and depth of your caves
but still, I remain

Under Covers

18

I don't understand
how your arms
could simultaneously hold me together
and make me fall apart

Comforting Solitude

Darkness echoed
The void filled with silence
Soft, slurred words drifting - fading into the
perplexing abyss of your mind
All sound of thought flowing -
slowly inching you toward a state of awakening
Your desires, secrets, and fears manifesting,
Crawling out of the obscurity of your
subconscious
Flickers of a soft moonlit glow sneaking through
your heavy eyes as it does a curtain being
swayed by the wind.
Your body surrendered, allowing you to fall
deeper into yourself as the sound of silence,
overwhelmed by peace and tranquility,
echoed through the night.

All I can give

To be a flower picked
A flower chosen
A beautiful rose to stick your nose in

Spreading love
And great devotion
For grief and friendship and deep emotion

To be a flower picked
A flower chosen
A blooming bud, cut and frozen

To bring you cheer
To bring you light
I wilt in silence so that you may take flight

To be a flower picked
A flower chosen
A blossom dead causes no commotion

And with the searing pain, of a dull-bladed knife
I gave you my color
I gave you my life.

I am a Waterfall

At a distance, you may gaze upon my beautiful
cascades
and bask in the glory of the sun reflecting on my
surface
You may lull yourself to sleep with the sounds of
my voice flowing endlessly
but ride my tides
and you will feel my force
Fall in my current
and you will drown under its pressure

65% Polyester, 35% mixed signals

I don't want to wear your sweater
I don't want to feel its warmth
And be embraced by its comfort

I don't want to wear your sweater
I don't want your scent to rub off on me
And become the familiar aroma of Home

I don't want to wear your sweater.
I don't want to feel safe under its soft black fabric
As if you cared enough to be there when I'm scared
Or sad
Or lonely

I don't want to wear your sweater.
I don't want to think that you let me keep it
because you like to see me in it.
Though my heart hopes you do

I don't want to wear your sweater.

I don't want the constant reminder that you do
not want to love me
The way I have grown to love you

Belides' Garden

To and fro we sway
"He loves me."
Down to the earth where the heartbroken lay
"He loves me not."
Tossed from above angels' white clouds
"He loves me."
Forming soft pillows upon the ground
"He loves me not."
One by one they pluck and pray
"He loves me."
A game, not all would dare to play
"He loves me not."
Hoping to another they may be bound
"He loves me."
My blossoms they pile all around
"He loves me not."
So should my last petal interrupt their flight
"He loves me."
they could fall upon my bed of white
"He loves..."

Smothered

25

My greatest desire
My darling
My fire

My greatest fear
With a flicker transpired

Alone I carried you
In solitude, I buried you
Never to meet
And unable to stay with you

My greatest desire
My darling
My fire

I loved you through death
and now grieve without tire